CREATIVE LIVING

CREATIVE LIVING

ERNEST HOLMES

Science of Mind Publications
Los Angeles, California

First Printing — October 1975
Second Printing — January 1978

Published by SCIENCE OF MIND PUBLICATIONS
3251 West Sixth Street • P.O. Box 75127
Los Angeles, California 90075

CONTENTS

FOREWORD

The twenty essays in this volume have been selected from the published and unpublished works of the late Ernest Holmes whose spiritual philosophy, Science of Mind, has meant so much to many tens of thousands around the world.

A variety of subjects are dealt with, and there is inspiration and wisdom in all of them. They can serve as guides to discovering a richer, fuller experience of living.

We do live in a spiritual universe, and the Infinite Intelligence which creates and sustains all is ever accessible to the individual for guidance once he becomes aware of It.

Science of Mind Publications

I
EMERGENCE

Nothing could have been more unexpected than that mutation, the "face turned from the clod," that is, a being with ideal vision; and yet the environment was prepared to give this most unpredictable "emergent" a welcome and a home when it arrived.

—RUFUS M. JONES

EVOLUTION

In the common medium of the Mind of God everything is individualized but at the same time it is Universal. There is some part of us that appears to be everywhere present. We are both Universal and individual at the same time because that which is Universal is the Presence that animates us, making us what we are, God in us. That which is individual is the manifestation of God in us as what we are.

We are normal, spontaneous, natural human beings in a process of unfolding, by means of error and truth. There is something about us that is terrific and eternal, but now but dimly seen, poorly discerned. Now we see as through a glass, darkly, but there is within each of us not only the eternal aspiration, but the absolute necessity of the continual expansion of the self.

No matter how imperfect we appear to be, God knows us as perfect, complete, divine, and the joy and delight of God Himself is in our act. Therefore, there is a Self beyond the self we know, understand, believe in, or have experienced. No man shall ever set us up or drag us down but ourselves, nor can anything rob us of happiness or we would not be free. The Self will raise the self by the self. It will grovel in the dust of its own creation or sit exalted on the mountaintop of its own illumination, and nothing shall stop it because we are individualizations of the Eternal.

It follows, then, that if God is peace we ought to be peaceful. If God is love, then we ought to experience that love and express it. If God is life, then there should be more of that life flowing through us. And if God is perfect, we ought to be more nearly perfect than we are. If there is hid within us a Divine incarnation of the living Spirit, and if no two persons are alike, then there is another fascinating concept possible. Each can know: I am one with God, I am one with everybody and all life, because God is one, but without being separated from the rest I am enough different that there is something in me which, if I will develop it, need not subsidize or compete but will express itself.

Every man is, in a sense, alone in the integrity of his own soul; no one can give to him but himself, and no one can take from him but himself. Under the great Law of God there is no law to him but his own soul shall set it. Do not two people view the same scene and one find it beauty and the other ugliness?

Every man lives more unto himself than he realizes. There is no man good enough and no man wise enough to have created his own life. And there is no man good enough or wise enough to destroy it.

Eternal evolution is a part of the principle that Jesus taught. He taught that all men are incarnations of God and that there is some way for every man to so know himself, to so see other men and other things that he would behold the eternal Creator in His creation.

LIFE

It seems as though everything in life is meant to circulate and the moment we stop the circulation that very act stagnates what would have moved freely. Stagnant water was once flowing water that became sidetracked from its own flow, and that which was perfect became impure.

It is just the same with our mind and our emotions. There is a pressure against us for self-expression, and when it is expressed our life flows happily, but when we tend to hinder it there is stagnation. The creative impulse must create something or we are unhappy.

All art, all invention, all creativity flows from a Divine source through the emotions and the intellect, and we do the best we can with it, blunderingly. Everything that is worthwhile is an effect of the feeling back of it. Back of all creativity is the pressure of our own Divinity to come forth into the humanity that It has created in order to enjoy the fullness of Its own expression.

The Universe is abundant, prolific with ideas, with intention, with volition, and with the power to execute. How could there be a star or a rosebud or the fertile imagination of a Shakespeare unless what we call Life pours Itself into all of them and is all of them?

Each one of us is a living God at the level of our human experience. Therefore, it must be that there is something in each one of us that sails on, as it were, into the Infinite, puts its feelers out eternally into the Infinite, and is always drawing back into our mind and experience as much as we can comprehend. There is Something in the universe that answers every one of us in the terms of the demand we make on It at the level of our capacity to understand It and our ability to become an instrument of It.

In the garden of our individual minds why should there not blossom love and friendship, abundance and success, and health and creativity without limit? But first we have to believe that it can happen; and second, we must properly identify ourselves with that Something so we may be instruments for Its operation.

If we could just identify ourselves with life and forget death, with love and forget hate, with joy and forget misery, with peace and forget discord, with abundance and forget limitation, how wonderful it would be. There has to come an awakening. Every man, in the simple integrity of his own individual soul, must learn to meet the Universe in exaltation.

There is nothing that Life could possibly withhold from Its creation since It has poured Its imagination and thought and feeling into everything, and spilled it over. The ocean of Life is forever flowing; we could just as well dip a gallon of water instead of a pint from It.

ENERGY

There is natural energy in the waterfall high in the mountains. We convert it, we channel it, we do not create it. We merely change it from a natural energy to mechanical power. Then we distribute it and attach it to that which we want it to operate. There is energy in the dynamic consciousness of the Divine Presence which we do not create; we convert it to the action of our thought and direct it for a definite and specific purpose through our word.

In this act of transforming the energy into power for specific action we are uniting an invisible Essence with an invisible Law, which is the way the universe operates. If we identify ourselves with the Source and perform the act, we may know that our word establishes eternal harmony, transforms everything, rearranges everything to our benefit. It is an act of complete surrender of the human to the Divine without the loss of the human. It is an act of complete inflowing of the Divine into the human without the limitation of the Divine.

If, knowing that the infinite Power is flowing through us, we still remain sick or unhappy or poor, we cannot blame God or man. Every time we say "I am" we are announcing the presence of omnipotent Power, which is God operating through our word. That is why we bring upon ourselves the thing we fear, or bring to ourselves the thing we desire.

The Power behind all things is, of Itself, without limit. It is All-Power; in us It becomes what we permit It to be. Our destiny is in our own hands. When we rise to an elevated state of consciousness where we see all things in their completeness, and know that an all-wise Power is behind it all, we will see that the Infinite could wish for us only that which expresses Itself in limitless terms.

It is now known that everything in the universe is in a state of flow. Emerson said that we view things as solid facts but God looks at them as liquid laws. The Universe does not toil, It flows. Should not each of us, then, stimulate himself to the act, not of intercession for the greater givingness of God, but for the more complete opening of the channel for the outflow of That which shall eternally inflow.

When we speak our word in the sanctuary of our own thought, in the independence and freedom of our own solitude, we are facing Reality, individually, with no man's opinion between. How much can any of us, in one brief moment or hour of time, come to sense and feel the impact of that Reality? That much will manifest! All the Power of the universe will be for it, and all the opinion of humanity cannot be against it. Here is where the soul faces the integrity of its own being, and knows God as that being.

POTENTIAL

Eternal unfoldment seems to be the law of our being. But what is it that unfolds? Is it the principle or the individuality? The answer is simple: we all know that principles do not evolve while persons do. Our evolution consists of the constant acquirement of knowledge leading to a more profound understanding of principles, but our understanding of principles does not create them. Principles are immutable, changeless, and eternal.

It should not seem strange that human endeavor should have discovered the principle of electrical energy. It should not seem strange that a principle of mental and spiritual power should have been discovered through the human mind. All the discoveries that have been made by man, and all the benefits accruing from these discoveries, have come through this channel.

When electricity was first discovered it seemed miraculous and to many the power of mind in action seems to work miraculously. We are too bound by superstition. When thunder broke, our ancestors thought the gods were angry or quarreling with each other, while the rainbow appeared to them to be the smile of the gods. Today an answered prayer is looked upon by many with awe as well as reverence, and many still think that God holds evil in store for the unbelieving.

Why should we look upon the manifestations of mind with superstition unless it is that we do not fully understand them? We now know that there is a Law which works on or through our word, thought, or belief. We know that faith and true prayer are actual channels through which the Law of Mind works. We know this because we have proved it sufficiently to be sure of the Law involved. The only way we can know any principle is from what it does and how it responds to our approach to it. There is nothing strange about this. The discovery of mind was made when man first began to think. The discovery of Spirit was made when man first realized that he was not alone in the universe.

Like all truths, when understood the truth about the spiritual power of thought is simple and may be approached directly. Truth is not something divulged to the elect by a jealous deity, nor is it given to a chosen few by direct revelation of a capricious God. We should resolutely brush aside all superstitions and discredit any attempt that may be made by anyone to cover that which will not be concealed.

We have a mind and are surrounded by and immersed in an infinite Intelligence. This is simple enough. We think, and thought is a force definitely directed. There is no mystery about this, anyone can understand it. Intelligent thought is directed energy. What makes it so? No one knows. *It is so.*

But there is more to it than this. Because energy does flow through thought, the more spiritual the thought the finer the results. What is spiritual thought? That kind of thought which believes that Good is the nature of the ultimate and absolute Power in the universe.

GROWTH

Nothing is static in the universe. It is only as that which we possess flows through us into the multiplication of itself, and the good it can do, that it can ever return as any good and lasting gratification. The Universe is in equal balance. To each one of us, because each one of us is an incarnation of God, the Universe reveals as much of Itself as we can see. There is already something within us which is transcendent and triumphant, not only eternal in the duration of time, but omnipresent in the now in which we live.

We view ourselves so finitely, so isolated,

so separated, that we do not seem to realize that the creative imagination of the Infinite is over all, in all, and through all, and the invisible and the visible are one.

There is what we call big, and what we call little. But the stars are not big, the atoms are not little, as substance, because they are identical; one is made up of a lot of the other. How can we say, then, that one man possesses more power than another? One man may use more power, but we all use the same Power. One man does not have greater joy than another; he may experience greater joy. Every man has access to all the joy there is.

If we could see this, if we could see that the relationship between the finite and the Infinite is in our own mind, we would know that there is no condemnation, no judgment, no restriction imposed upon us by the eternal Presence.

We may have batted our heads against a stone wall yesterday. We may have been like a fish which left the ocean of its infinity and swam up what looked like a limitless passageway which became narrower and narrower until at last the fish was thrashing itself against the confines of that which alone could liberate it if it reversed its course and returned to the sea from which it sprang.

Technology has given us the modern conveniences that we all enjoy, but the world is more insecure than it ever was because it has detached itself from the spiritual center and wanders alone and is lost in the midst of unbelief. Therefore there is something missing in the accomplishment of human endeavor.

We are on the pathway of an everlasting and ever-expanding evolution, but it could be much more rapid if we would only surrender the whole idea of separation and isolation, and discipline ourselves to the thought and the act of meeting that which is desirable in every person and every situation.

Let us not wait, individually. There is a doorway to which the history of the human race and all the great leaders may lead us, but the door cannot be opened from the outside. It must be opened by that which has been described as the High Priest within us. The Eternal is not static in the temporal, the Infinite is not bound by the finite, nor is God restricted by man. The slightest act of ours, like the atom, can be multiplied into the aggregate of the magnitude of man.

II

EXPERIENCE

Life and spirit are two powers or necessities, between which man is placed. Spirit gives meaning to his life, and the possibility of the greatest development. But life is essential to spirit, since its truth is nothing if it cannot live.

—CARL G. JUNG

FREEDOM

We are all sandwiched at this moment between all that has happened in the past and all that is going to happen in the future. But nature is very wise. If all the sorrow and grief we have suffered through the past were to come to us and bear down upon our consciousness in this moment, there is no one of us who could stay sane for thirty seconds. And it would be just as impossible for us to stand the elation and ecstasy of all the joy we have ever had, could it be crowded into one brief moment.

Nature has provided that as experiences

stream away from us they enter what we call memory, and memory becomes what we call an automatic tendency toward the future. The past, then, is a living thing because it promotes the present. The future is a living thing because it becomes the present. But the past, the present, and the future are merely like taking an elastic band and stretching it out and then bringing it together again. It is merely the evolution of consciousness and the unfoldment of action.

We cannot wipe out yesterday as though it had no existence and dissolve memory, which is the only thing that acts as a link of continuity threading one experience on another. On the other hand, yesterday cannot have any existence as though it existed of itself, because it is now passed. Therefore, the impulsions of yesterday carried over into today are creating today, and the reactions of today are creating our tomorrows.

If it were possible to short-circuit, as it were, the time track of yesterday that was unhappy and morbid, and if yesterday is not a thing in itself or of itself but only a memory which is alive, the only place we can do that is right where we are. Yesterday is active only because of our reaction to it; it is that which is and is not. It is where it ought to be but mostly we have put it where it should not be. Suppose a man fails. He is disappointed and the chagrin and emotional reaction of defeat submerge him. He cannot wipe out his memory but he can think about what is going on now, what he is going to do today.

For instance, if there is a great ice jam overflowing the banks of a river, when the sun comes up its warmth does not try to reconcile the fact that a lot of frozen water is holding back a lot of unfrozen water, because they are both water anyway. The warmth of the sun transmutes, that is, it melts the ice. It does not argue with it, does not fight it. It changes it. Therefore, there is a spiritual attitude of thought that does not have to deal with our psychological or physiological problems. It recognizes them and without fighting these attitudes, will transmute and transform them.

As we look back over our yesterdays we need not be afraid to face them and meet every unpleasant situation, but to know that there is nothing in the Universe that can operate against us or what we are doing; that everything that was good in yesterday shall perpetuate itself, nothing else can be active in us. And as we do this the unhappy memories will be transmuted into happiness, and there will be a new freedom in living.

SECURITY

There can be nothing worthwhile in life without security. Not just financial security, but a larger security, no longer being afraid of the universe, no longer being afraid of tomorrow or morbidly thinking of what happened yesterday.

The man who lives in the past is carrying an impossible load and the man who lives only in the future is carrying an idle dream. The happiness that brings a feeling of security is the happiness we get out of today.

There is no security without faith, a faith

in Life, one free from fear. We have never, any of us, had enough good or enough happiness, but the moment we say it is individual rather than individualized, the moment we seek to cut our good off from the whole good, that moment we hug it with fear to our bosoms, then someone stronger than we will surely snatch it from us.

What is war? Fear! What is hatred? Fear! What is intolerance? Fear! Fear of what? Of the world we live in, and of God. Fear arising partly out of the past and partly out of contemplation of the future, because the past is largely molding the consciousness today.

We have to be free from self-condemnation or condemnation of the world or other people, because our condemnation of others is very much a projection of our unconscious condemnation of ourselves. We must have faith in ourselves, in life, and in God. Every man is his own success or failure story.

In such degree as we develop the ability to see joy everywhere, everywhere joy will come back to us. In such degree as we have the ability to see honesty, it will respond to us. In such degree as we flow along with the eternal currents of our being everything is made easy. But in such degree as we try to swim against the current of Life we are contradicting Its Divine influx and even God, as far as we are concerned, cannot seem to pass through the door of our mind when it is closed.

It does not matter what happened yesterday; the history of a tale that is told does not matter. There is a truth, known today, that is transcendent of all our yesterdays and wipes them out. There is nothing wrong with today if we live it rightly, and no moment in eternity will be any better than the one in which we live now.

The first part of wisdom is to accept the miracle of Life and know that only faith is real and God is not an illusion. How wonderful would be the path of self-expression if we were no longer afraid. But if we want to feel secure in our lives today we must come to know that we are one with all Life — the song of the lark, the rush of the wind, the strength of the wave, the beauty of the sunset, the glory of the dawn; that all creation enters into us as we enter into the heart of the Universe which is wondrous kind.

How wonderful to know that today may be a fresh beginning. What a sense of security to feel at last that we are in the arms of an infinite Intelligence, Its offspring.

SUCCESS

If we believe, absolutely, that we can do a certain thing the way will always be opened for us to do it. If we believe that time has to elapse before we can achieve it, then we are making that a law, and time will have to elapse. If, on the other hand, we believe that Divine Mind knows just how to do it and never makes mistakes, and we accept this action, then it will be done now.

We cannot imagine the Spirit hurrying or worrying, fretting or trying to make anything happen. The only reason we worry and fret is because we have not realized that there is but

One Power for good in the universe and we are always using It, but using It according to our belief. This is our Divine birthright; nothing hinders us but ourselves.

How limited we are! How little our thought! Much of the human race rises in the morning, plods off to the day's work, plods home at night, sore and tired, eats and sleeps, works and dies. This was never intended. It is the result of man's belief in two powers, one of good and one of evil. There has to come a greater vision and to those who believe and act as though this vision were true now, it will prove true in their lives.

There is nothing selfish with wanting to be successful in all that we do. It would be selfish only if we had to rob someone else to attain it. We will be of value to the world, or to ourselves, only in such degree as our lives are happier and more fulfilled.

We should expect the best to happen. One who has learned to trust the Universe will not be surprised even when he finds things coming from the most unexpected sources. All things are man's to use and then to let go of. What more can we ask? We want nothing that we have to keep; things are to use, not to hold. We should expect that everything is to come our way, and be content and cheerful if we wish to attract our good from the store of the Infinite. We should open our whole consciousness to the greater possibilities of life, accept our greater good.

We cannot stand still. If we want to do something new we must get a new concept and then the Law of Mind will provide the circumstances which will make for the fulfillment of our desire. We must get over the old idea of limitation, overcome all precedents, and set ourselves in the new order of things. If we want to build a railroad, we will never do it unless we overcome the idea that the most we can hope for in life is small things. When we realize that God has created us for a glorious future we can dare to fling out into Mind the great assurances about our individual fulfillment.

Because we have not yet arrived at a complete acceptance of the supremacy of good we have to do the best we can. But we have to hitch our earthly wagon to a spiritual star, because if we do not we are going to hitch it to a make-believe life, something that offers no possibility of advancement. We ought to so live and think that our expectancy of successful living is not interfered with.

ABUNDANCE

Everywhere we look we see that nature is lavish, abundant, extravagant. Nothing is ever lost to God; everything that manifests goes back into an unmanifest state to appear again in a different form. No matter how much we take out of the Universe, if we take out with one hand we have to put back with the other because the Universe is everywhere and it is one system.

We need a big concept of the Universe. We need to know that all substance will remain the same, in essence, including the laws that govern it. The form it takes is never twice alike, and does not have to be, because there is always enough continuity in each expression to keep its form in harmony and symmetry.

There is one Substance in the Universe. It takes the form of the supply we need, when we need it. I believe that there are great cosmic patterns to which we are attached. One of them is what in our language we call substance, which in our human limited sense means supply and right action. There is one Mind that knows everything, and that Mind knows in us. Therefore, when we accept Its guidance we are compelled to choose rightly and act upon our choice to acquire those things we have need of.

There can never be the proper circulation of Substance as supply to humanity until the Divine pattern is recognized. Why should we go through life impoverished in spirit? Everywhere we see the greater good held away because of a denial of a lesser good, and because we think there is no other avenue through which money or affection or appreciation can come. It is hard to gain spiritual maturity, to see that God is in everything because God is all there is.

What the whole world has believed operates through us, but we are not aware of it. So we should not be surprised that we all are carrying around with us thoughts that deny the supremacy of good. However, we know that one kind of thought can erase another. Otherwise, if we are full of negative thoughts and they are attracting negative conditions, and if we could not change them, then we would be caught in a trap. Fortunately, this is not the case.

It has been proved in scientific demonstrations that no matter how much anybody has failed, if he can affirm success he can neutralize the failure. If we can come to know that one kind of thought will neutralize another, wipe it out, then we can set about to change our thinking and our world of experience.

Whoever lifts his cup of acceptance to the outpouring of the Divine abundance shall find that it will be filled. But mostly we turn the cup upside down. Whoever strives and spends time enough, gets away long enough from the confusion of life, will discover a new experience of abundant living.

HAPPINESS

What does happiness mean? First of all,
there is no happiness unto the self alone. No
one was born to be lonely nor was he born to
be alone. If God had needed only one of us
that is all He would have made. He evidently
needed a lot of us and a very great variety,
and that is what He made. And God never
made a mistake. God would not have made all
these infinite variations unless God were one
Life, one Power, one Presence, expressing
Himself in innumerable forms and person-
alities.

There is no happiness unto the self alone.

It is impossible. Every day we see people try it, only to find that happiness eludes them. There is no happiness unto just our family alone. We seem to be afraid to love more people for fear we will love the few less. That is not true. It is only when we love all more that we love few better. That does not mean that we should exclude our family, but that we should include a larger family and reach out and embrace everything and everybody. Only those people who have done this have known complete bliss.

There is no happiness without fulfillment and there is no fulfillment except in such degree as we loose the natural energies of the physical, the mental, and the spiritual elements of our being. The Spirit within us is infinite Love, but when we deny Its flow to another we are inhibiting Its action in us.

Always we are confronted with this stupendous fact: It is our littleness that obscures the larger vision. If we look at a sunset, then place our little hands in front of our little eyes — it is all gone. What a little thing obscures a big thing! It is the little things of life that destroy us. We should become more inclusive and there is no other way to do it other than by spiritual conviction. Everything else has failed.

There is no good or bad in the universe as God sees it; there is no right or wrong as God sees it. There is only what is. And it is harmony and beauty and peace and joy and happiness. But that which we refuse to offer to another we cannot take and God cannot force it upon us. The pressure for self-expression which is back of everything, the distinctive self-awareness that every living being has, must be expressed but it can only be expressed as it joins hands with the whole world.

Life is made to live and we want to be

happy and whole, but it is impossible to the self alone. Forevermore something sings, not unto you or unto me but unto each other. We cannot only embrace ourselves; somehow our arms must find themselves around the shoulders of all humanity. We cannot worship a God who belongs to us alone. Only as we enter into a feeling of the Essence that diffuses Itself everywhere, then at last we can look at each other and say, "I worship God in your form."

This is happiness. It will not come in fragments. We may try to make a bargain with it as though we would save ourselves. But it calls for a complete surrender.

III

EXPRESSION

The highest is in all of us. At times it flames up and we know that we are not dust but spirit, and that in fellowship with the Spiritual Life from whence we came, is our power and our peace.

—HARRY EMERSON FOSDICK

CREATIVITY

There is only one creative Law in the universe operating automatically upon everything, creating a form for every idea that is given to It. Once the only growth in the desert was cactus, sagebrush, or whatever seed the wind blew or the birds dropped. The creative Law acting upon the soil did not ask the direction of the wind or the kind of birds; It merely set to work to create a form which would correspond with the pattern that impregnated It. It did not ask if it was good or bad, big or little.

This same creative Law made the giant

sequoia and the little buttercup; It made the flea and the elephant; It made the grain of sand and the vast sidereal universe of galaxies and nebulae.

The only difference between the natural desert and the cultivation of it was not in the sun and the air and the soil, but in what was done with it. The growth was accomplished by a neutral agency ready to spring forth into blossoming of the peach tree just as it had in the creation of the cactus. And so it is with all life.

A businessman has an idea, he thinks up a way of doing things. He is using the creative Law just as much as an artist who paints a picture. We speak of creative arts and creative people, but we fail to realize that all life deals with creativity. There is no big or little, no important or unimportant. To the creative Law there is no difference between a child making mud cakes or an engineer building a bridge.

We do not create in the sense that we make something out of nothing, but only in the sense that we make something out of something. And we create a new form because we are equipped with a mind to think and to feel and to will and to imagine. So everyone who makes a demand on spiritual Law will cause the Law to respond in the only way It can — in the terms of the demand made.

There is a creative Intelligence in the universe that acts exactly like the soil does physically, but It is a spiritual thing. It is a universal Mind Principle responding to us as Law, operating upon our thoughts the way we think them, apparently. We do not know how or why It reacts to us, but we do know that It does; we have to accept It.

Whoever thinks about something will draw

into his consciousness the elements of that thing about which he thinks. Whoever, as he thinks, believes this will happen will hasten the process and clarify and amplify it by and through his consent, consciously given, no matter what it is.

Every one of us personally has back of us the potential of the Universe. There is an irresistible potential pressing against everyone for self-expression. If we listen we shall hear it, not as a voice, but as a feeling, as a Divine urge to express. If we believe in it, it shall manifest through us, and if we keep our consciousness active and alive to it, the volume that flows through us by our consent will necessarily increase. But we have to believe that it will.

LOVE

In its broadest sense love is the impartation of the self, the givingness of everything we are or hope to be or have, and giving it in joy and without reservation in complete abandonment. Unfortunately, in our present stage of evolution it seems that we can only do this with a very few people. Our horizon is too close to our eyes; perhaps it shuts out more than it ever shuts in. We have a vast estate in the Universe which we have not even ventured into for fear we would be lost like a bird that has spent its life in a little cage and feels lost if put in a tree outdoors; everything is too big for it to comprehend.

One of the greatest needs of the human being is to be loved. We would not have this need if love were not the greatest thing in the world. Without love we cannot live. But mostly we pick out only a few people upon whom to lavish our love. If we loved everybody more should we love a few less? It is something we have to learn.

Whenever there is a deep sense of being rejected or not loved there comes with it an outer aggressive attitude, a combativeness. For when love does not flow out, aggression seems to take its place. People in adult life who are always wondering what others think about them, or feel that they are not accepted by society, become what we call antisocial, and are generally those who lacked proper affection in childhood. The life without love is unfulfilled, always seeming to carry around with it the burden of rejection and too often becoming moody and morose as well as unhappy.

Where fear, hate, suspicion, and a lack of confidence may have blocked us, the flowing out of love produces an opposite effect. For love always liberates, it always increases our livingness. But love remains empty until it gives of itself. It is not, then, love of the self that we need, but the givingness of the love from the self that opens up the healing channels of life, not only in our minds and emotions, but in our physical bodies and in our affairs. Whenever we meet people through whom love shines, a unity is formed, harmony is produced, and we desire to be in their presence.

We should, then, take such love as we have in our hearts today and freely give it to everyone we meet. If it seems rejected by some, we should not be hurt, driven back into our prison, but remain liberated. If we do this we shall find a reaction in our physical bodies nothing less than miraculous, for love can restore circulation, heal the heart as well as the mind, and give speed to hands and feet as well as to thought.

Love will find the solution to every problem, will answer every question. It is the lodestone of life, the center of reality, the heart of the universe, and it will ultimately win and vanquish every foe.

Love begets tolerance, and tolerance begets understanding, which is being able to put oneself in the other person's place and see why he acts as he acts, why he does what he does. Thus love can create a better world in which to live. It is the one Power which can and must bring peace to a changing world.

GIVINGNESS

Life undoubtedly belongs to the ones who take it. But how can we take it unless we first give it? It is impossible. So true givingness is the transmitting of the self to everything we do, it does not matter what it is — the out-pouring of ourself into every undertaking with an enthusiastic zest, love, kindness, and friendliness.

It is a fundamental law of mental polarity, cause and effect, that that which goes out comes back the way it went out, plus the in-tensification of that which it has contacted en-route. If we dislike someone he will feel it, no matter what we say. Then whatever there is in him that dislikes anything or anyone intensifies our dislike for him and creates an unconscious desire in him to dislike us.

Why is there antagonism and resistance? It is because we are giving lip service. In reality we cannot fool God or each other. There is something in us that knows the real from the false. It is because in the universe we cannot set up a camouflage. There is an all-penetrating eye, an all-hearing ear, an all-knowing mind, and we cannot resist the inevitabilities of the law of our own being. We should withhold every gift unless we wish to make it. We can make no bargains with Life. We should give only when the gift and the giver are one and the same thing. If we want to get the most from life we can only do it as we have first given the most of ourselves, then the response comes back to us multiplied.

God is the original giver. Life gives by imparting Itself to the object of Its desire. But how could there be a givingness unless there were an equal acceptance? We must set up a receiving center. No matter how abundantly the horn of plenty may pour out its universal gifts, we must hold up our bowl of acceptance or the gift cannot be complete. Life is ready to give us all that we desire, but we must first cast from us everything that hinders Its complete expression through us; let go of all struggle and strife, and accept the Divine bounty. Then we must be willing to share that which we have received.

We should allow the gifts of Life to flow out to everything we touch, everyone we meet, every situation we contact. Then, wherever we go every situation is blessed, every person is helped, every discord is harmonized, without our even being conscious of it. Just as automatically as we cast a shadow we can so train the mind that automatically something shall flow from us to bless everything in our world. This would be the supreme gift.

Each of us is the only person, in a certain sense, that we shall ever know. Ours are the only eyes, spiritually, mentally, and physically, that we have to look through. It should be our purpose and desire that everything we touch shall spring into its own resurrection, revealing its own eternal day, through the guidance and the eternal givingness of God.

PEACE

No matter how much we seek to attach our troubles to God, God is never troubled. God does not, as it were, come down and enter into our troubles to straighten them out. If He did He would be more confused than we are because He has more to be confused with, but there is no such thing as Cosmic confusion.

Reality abides in eternal peace, in everlasting calm. Consequently, we cannot carry our confusion into peace any more than we could carry darkness into light. But if we could let go of our confusion long enough to receive the peace, as the light shines in the darkness and dissipates it, so the peace would dissipate the confusion and it would not be there.

We have to let go of our problem long enough to take hold of the answer or to at least be receptive to it. It is the nature of every disease to heal itself. It is well known psychologically that it is the nature of every mental pain to soothe its own anguish, so we may be sure that the pressure of God's Power is so great against all things that if we open but the smallest crack the winds of heaven will fill our sails with a dynamic power that shall surely carry our boat into a safe harbor.

Since God is the reality of each of us, there is a part of us that has no problems. Our individual being does not contradict the equilibrium of the universe. Man is the only thing that is confused; nature is not. If we slaughter each other, the grass will still be green, water will still be wet, everything will still go on.

We are not lost but often we do not know where we are. That is a different thing. It has to do with our lack of realization that the Universe could not exist for one split second if It were confused or operating against Itself. It does not matter how bad anything looks in our experience, there is beyond that Something that can heal it.

We have to believe in the transcendent Power, then we have to believe we can hook up with It because we are already one with It. Then we have to believe that when we speak our word we are tapping the source of infinite Harmony at a level higher than the finite discord, therefore our word of authority will take precedence over the discord.

There is such a thing, then, as reaching a state of consciousness above the level of our confusion and in such degree as we do that there is no argument, no controversy, no confusion; there is no fear, no doubt, no uncertainty. We should seek an awareness of the infinitude and stillness of the everlasting Peace, the motion of the ceaseless Energy that flows through everything in majestic calm. We must believe that there is within us a pattern of living beyond all confusion, beyond all fear, and that it is here and now because the Universe in which we live is here and now. We must seek to feel it.

PRAYER

Since we know we cannot do anything to God — God is most certainly not influenced by our thinking — then we know prayer must do something to ourselves, and what we do has to be mental, a thing of thought. What can it be other than that we ourselves believe? That is really the secret of effective prayer.

Jesus taught about prayer: ". . . as thou hast believed, so be it done unto thee." This is the mental assumption, the attitude we assume in mind, and consequently when we pray or give a spiritual treatment something will happen which will exactly correspond to our mental state of acceptance and embodiment. It will correspond through the person, the place, or the thing with which we identify our word, treatment, or prayer.

Consequently, all things are possible with faith, in such degree as faith first is real and is in accord with the laws of being. We cannot change God, but our faith can change us. It does not influence God; it merely measures out more of God to us in the way that we believe, and our belief is the measurer-outer.

Faith and fact must unite else we are living in a world of illusion. God's world cannot be a world of illusion but must be one of eternal verities. We can never deny a fact to establish a faith.

There can be no problem that cannot be solved unless we assume that Divine Intelligence does not know what It is doing. We must realize that every human problem, whether it is personal or the problem of the survival of civilization, is not a problem that cannot be solved, but merely one that has not been solved because it has not been properly presented to the Intelligence that knows everything. The Universe is one system and if any prayer has ever been answered since time began there was a principle, a law operating, and a way through which and by which it happened. And if anyone can understand it and use it, he will be able to prove it and it will work. To understand spiritual truths and to prove them by the evidence of something happening is the only proof we have. If faith is a power, it will do something.

The trouble with too many people is that they want somebody else to think for them, they want to live by the authority of other people and never get to be something themselves. God has to respond to us at the level of our acceptance of God. This is the principle of faith and the reaction of that principle to our belief.

We cannot live without faith because faith is real. There is ever pressing against us the dynamic force of That which paints the sunset and causes the soft glow of the evening twilight, sings in the bird and plays in the child, and proclaims Itself at the level of our recognition of It. Every man is an outlet for the Divine. We should recognize this and embody it in our every thought and act.

IV

EMINENCE

We are part of an alive, vibrant universe where the true reality is spirit. When we learn to live in harmony with this spirit, and catch its rhythm, then we will be in tune with power as never before.

—NORMAN VINCENT PEALE

UNIQUENESS

We all belong to the human race but there is something a little different about each one of us. God is not different because we are different, but He does a unique thing through us. God presents Himself to each of us *through* us in a way that will never be reproduced again. We should acknowledge it and identify our intellect and emotions with this intense creativity.

There is an intensity of concentrated creativity and imagination that will expand and burst the seed, crowd aside the soil, send down roots, send up shoots, and create an oak tree to shelter the birds and give shade to the animals and reproduce and multiply itself perennially, ad infinitum. This dynamic action is at the center of everything and everyone. The intimate relationship we have with the Infinite is a relationship with a dynamic Power, a creative Intelligence, a deathless Being, and something that is eternally in a state of intense activity.

Our personality is the objective mental and emotional reaction to this unique relationship. Our personality we create and develop; as we change it fluctuates, up and down. It is the personality that tries to imitate; it is the personality that tries to influence; it is the personality that takes up an aggression and tries to fight because it is hurt. It is the isolated person who feels afraid of the universe and of God; he does not dare to die and has not the courage to live.

We all have many faces, many moods when the personality is hiding the individualization. But through all of these many faces of the personality there is flowing the essential essence of the living Spirit, the ocean of Life pouring out through this living stream. Each of us shall reach the ocean again in the eternal circuits of God, but never to the loss of our identity.

Consequently, we can develop the personality, rightly and permanently, only as in thought, imagination, feeling, we tie it back to a unique individualization. We should realize that all the energy, action, vitality, enthusiasm, and purposiveness that there is in the universe is flowing through us. We should gladly open our consciousness to it and it will flow through everything we think, say, or do. As we reach back into the fullness of the stature of that which is incarnated in us we can, through recognizing the Divinity, redeem the humanity.

Every man should accept himself. Not necessarily the confused self, the self that is afraid, but he must identify this smaller self with the Self that God created.

There is always the actor before the action, the creator before that which is created which stands in a unique relationship to the Creator of all that is. God must express Himself. We are His expression. We must also be His delight. This is the real person, this is what we are.

EMOTIONS

Every person, place, and thing has a definite atmosphere. The thought and emotion centered in or around a location permeates it with an atmosphere which is consciously or unconsciously felt by all who approach it. This is even more evident in the personal atmosphere. It is impossible for a person to conceal his joy or sorrow, his likes or dislikes, his beliefs or fears, for the unexpressed word speaks a language as clear and definite as the spoken.

A whole community shudders with horror over an atrocious or criminal act. Likewise, a whole community may enter into the spirit of a fiesta and laugh easily at the most trivial of jokes. A whole nation may feel the depression of financial stringency, the enthusiasm of a presidential contest, or the horror of a world war. Thought waves pass through the minds of all who are receptive to them and influence these minds in such degree as they are receptive.

The power in people that attracts or repels is almost entirely mental and spiritual. An active and dynamic mind creates activity wherever it goes, while mental drowsiness has the reverse effect. Since these things are true, and since we may all learn to control our thinking and govern our emotions, it follows that anyone may surround himself with an atmosphere of happiness, of peace, of enthusiasm, and of right action, thus drawing to his center those things which make life worthwhile.

We feel sad as we enter into the thought

or come under the spell of the emotion of those who are depressed. Why should it not be possible to remain poised in our own mind, certain in our own thought, and peaceful in the midst of confusion? We shall some day learn to sympathize with others, to love and help them, without falling under the mesmeric spell of their emotions. We should analyze our own mental reactions and ascertain what emotions or intellectual concepts we are responding to, and why. We should definitely determine what position we are to take and positively maintain that position, disregarding any apparent contradiction. In this way alone can we truly remain an individual in the midst of the collective consciousness of the human race.

The average person is more or less hypnotized from the cradle to the grave, does not know what he believes, or why, has no definite concepts of his own and is compelled to go through life lacking that positive individuality and that definite power of personal conviction which is the Divine birthright of every individual.

To those few rare individuals who have somewhat penetrated beyond the objective surface and discovered the spiritual cause of things we instinctively turn, for they have brought to us the atmosphere of another country, news from heaven and water from the eternal reservoir.

DESIRE

The subjective state of our mind is like the wild oats that grow in abundance on the hills in Southern California. The oats come up automatically because that is all that is put into the soil. Then the seeds that automatically fall perennially from the old crop reseed the hills. All the thoughts and ideas we have had all of our life are like these perennial plants, they reseed themselves.

We cannot change the fact that whatever we put into mind will be reflected back to us. But we can change that which is reflected. We can uproot the old, we can implant the new, we can neutralize what is already there.

If we are tending a garden we can pull up unwanted plants and plant others in their places; if we are painting a picture we can paint out certain things and paint in new; if we are building a building and there is something we do not like, we can rebuild it. If we could not uproot the old and implant the new we should be caught in the old and we should be subject to its endless and monotonous repetition.

If we want to be free from suffering we have to stop inflicting it. If we want love we have to love, no matter what anybody thinks of us. If we no longer want to be condemned we must no longer condemn somebody else. Without harm, without hurt, we may liberate ourselves and help to liberate others, lifting ourselves by the power of our creative imagination to the consciousness of the omnipotence of good and the omnipresence of the living Spirit.

Our desire will come to us only when we understand it and when we incorporate it into our own consciousness. Then it will gradually become subjectified. That which is subjective will become automatic and that which is automatic will bring to us from the farthest corners of the world the good we did not know was coming but was already incorporated in the good we expected.

We have to separate the difference between the desire and the deep thought that reacts to it. We can desire a thing so badly that it almost paralyzes us and still believe we are not going to have it. Therefore, our hope and desire must pass into the certainty of acceptance, and acceptance into an atmosphere of embodiment, a complete realization that this is the way it is.

Deserting that which would contradict this, and still feeling coming up out of old experience those things that deny the good we desire, we must reaffirm the presence of the ideal. Then as time passes, a little here and a little there, the images will change and gradually the very concepts within us which used to attract sadness now will attract joy. If we can get it firmly in our minds that there is nothing in the Universe that wishes us evil, there is nothing in the Universe that desires to limit us, then everything will conspire to bring to us that which we desire because we are the delight of the living God, right now.

FRIENDSHIP

There is something in us that is akin to every person who ever lived and if we would meet people without embarrassment, having nothing to "put over" and knowing that we do not need to take anything away from anyone, then we would meet people on the terms of spiritual equality. This is the basis of friendship.

There is a common meeting ground between people but we cannot enter that common meeting ground while we hold someone away from us, no matter what the pretense is. If we say, "He is more highly educated than I," or, "Look at his social position!" we do not dare to meet him. That is called an inferiority complex. On the other hand, if we feel that he is less worthy than we are, that is called a superiority complex. Both find their roots in the common belief of inadequacy.

What are we looking for in people? Probably we are bringing out pretty much what we are looking for. Our own states of consciousness reacting within ourselves silently attract that which is like them. We must not think of people as better or worse. All people are all right if we meet them in an all-right way, and we shall bring out of a person whom we meet that which is like the subjective acceptance of the life we live. The adage that "birds of a feather flock together" is true, and it is natural that we should draw people to us who appear to like the same things.

If we want to get the most out of our friendships and enjoy each other the most there is only one way: we never get the most until we give the most. We should not be afraid of the inward conviction, the emotional sense that belongs to all life which would cause us to love to embrace all humanity. The person who can embrace only a few is merely limiting his vision of the greater possibility. What God has included we had better not try to exclude. The individual who has learned to love all people will find plenty of people who will return that love to him.

We could not know that each other exists if we were completely separate and isolated individuals. Because there is One Mind or Spirit, which is God, we can recognize each other. Therefore, that within us which is Universal recognizes that which is individual. When there is a conscious union of the person with the Universal that recognition is exhilarated and extended.

There is no person in the world in whom we could not find delight if we knew him in the right way. Everyone wants and needs friendship. The man who does not desire friendship is mentally maladjusted to life. The happiest man is the man who gets along with people. There has never yet been a case of a person who changed his belief in isolation to friendship who did not become a friend.

IMMORTALITY

The first law of our life is self-preservation. Therefore, we want to know: If a man dies, shall he live again? Is this whole experience of living a vast panorama of tragedy and pain and fear to be climaxed by the final exit of nothing to nothing? Or is it the working out of a great and glorious program, the significance of which, as we view it, causes the little suffering we have had to fall into a different place entirely, like when a child stubs its toe and we pick it up and say, "There, there, in a minute you'll be all right," and it is.

It would be a contradiction to say that both life and death proceed from the same principle. One is the repudiation of the other. We know by intuition that there is something beyond what we have experienced in this world. There are moments in the life of all when the veil seems thin between and we almost enter into the heavenly state. We are living in an eternal moment longer than our temporal one, but we are still in the awakening process.

All the tomorrows that stretch down the vistas of eternity will be but a continuity of our own experiences. We shall keep on keeping on. We shall continue in our individual stream of consciousness but forever and ever expanding. Not less but ever more, more, and still more. Everything in our lives is new at all times. It is now held by science that there is not an atom of our physical body that was here a year ago. If this is true of our physical body, we have no reason to doubt that it may be true of the structure of our spiritual existence. Back of everything is that Life which forevermore makes everything new.

Immortality is a principle in Life. All people are immortal or no one is immortal. Fortunately, we now know that all people are, and that each leaves this world taking the only thing with him that he can take — his spirit, his mind, his consciousness. This is the one eternal reality of the inner self. No doubt evolution will continue beyond the grave, for man is an expanding, eternally evolving and unfolding principle of Life.

The spirit which at our birth came from the Invisible into the experience of this earthly life constitutes the one great reality, and its ongoingness at the end of this earthly span is all that matters. The soul is the only triumphant, deathless, and unconquerable thing we possess. What we call death is only an expansion of the soul, an enlargement of experience, a gateway into higher expressions of life and truth.

We should be aware of the immortality of our own souls here and now. We should know that we are the beloved of God, the offspring of Eternity, sons of the living Spirit, born of eternal day. This is the great truth of our being: that we are forever individualizing the Spirit. Why, then, should we not enter into the spirit of our immortality, right now? Why wait to die?